APERTURE

Ansel Adams, *Road After Rain*, North Coast, Northern California, 1960

Photographs by Ansel Adams, Robert Adams, Lewis Baltz, Virginia Beahan
and Laura McPhee, H. H. Bennett, Marilyn Bridges, Wynn Bullock, Evelyn
Cameron, Paul Caponigro, John Cliett, William Clift, Lois Conner, Lynn Davis,
Robert Dawson, Peter Gasser, David Gibson, Laura Gilpin, Frank Gohlke,
Nancy Goldring, F. J. Haynes, Wanda Hammerbeck, William Henry Jackson,
Nicholas Kahn and Richard Selesnick, Barbara Kasten, Robert Glenn Ketchum,
Stuart Klipper, Koichiro Kurita, Tseng Kwong Chi, Dorothea Lange, Steve
Lawson, Sally Mann, Richard Misrach, Eadweard Muybridge, Joan Myers,
Herman Nielson, Timothy O'Sullivan, Philipp Scholz Rittermann, Stephen
Shore, Art Sinsabaugh, Paul Strand, Jerry N. Uelsmann, Carleton E. Watkins,
Brett Weston, and Minor White.

D1384344

MOMENTS OF GRACE: SPIRIT IN THE AMERICAN LANDSCAPE

While belief in a god as an undeniable reality or as an abstract concept is often in debate, many people believe in or sense an otherness—something beyond the influence of human beings, either outward or inward, surely intangible but reachable, at moments—to be an inherent factor in humankind's experience. These "moments of grace," these so-called epiphanies, when we are enriched in spirit and knowledge, are more or less intuitive perceptions or insights into the reality or essential meaning of something. Everyone has them—minute glimpses of awareness or profound breakthroughs of revelation, most of which are simply assimilated into ourselves, into our unconscious cores. Others, more memorable perhaps, linger in our conscious selves. It can be argued, in the purest sense, that epiphanies are solely personal experiences, the essence and magnitude of which defy description. Yet, perhaps the arts in general, and photography in particular, can most tangibly and sublimely suggest these moments of acute awareness.

Photographers have described a "moment of grace," when they are unexpectedly able to create an image of lasting meaning and revelation. Though such experiences are evoked by time and place they nevertheless transcend the immediate and personal, bringing to light a timeless and universal awareness which previously may have been only a dim shadow.

What *Aperture* is exploring as a "moment of grace"—be it the photographer's, the effect of the photograph on the viewer, or both—is not confined to the religious. These moments may evoke a sense of freedom, individuality, well-being, peacefulness, timelessness, isolation, dread, horror, terror, anger, or hate. They may suggest our uniqueness, confirm our part in a whole, instill in us a godhead or determine its absence. There is no narrow definition of this theme in this issue. The images selected may be the result of a photographer waiting hours or weeks for the elements to combine in a manner that precipitates a transcendental event, or they may be invented images which convey this heightened awareness in other ways.

Robert Adams said, "We rely on landscape photography to make intelligible to us what we already know. It is the fitness of the landscape to one's experience of life's condition and possibilities that finally make a scene important to us." The American landscape represents the universal gifts nature has bestowed and, at the same time, it can be seen as a textbook for our successes and failures to live and prosper with dignity within its realms.

"Moments of Grace" presents a selection of photographs that reveal deeply felt personal responses to the landscape. Although the selection does not canvass the history of landscape photography, certain divisions arise in the way photographers over the years have responded to the land. This issue is divided into four sections which offer both divergent and convergent approaches.

The work of early photographers such as Timothy O'Sullivan, Carleton E. Watkins, and Eadweard Muybridge was at first documentary in intention. They were awed when confronted with a wilderness seemingly unruly and clearly unrestricted by man; nature had the upper hand. Today, we are hard put to see nature as an independent, omnipotent force. Bill McKibben writes in this issue that humankind, by our use of fossil fuels and the spread of pollutants, has so altered the patterns of weather and climate in which we live that we, in effect, now determine the character of nature. Nature has become a by-product of our transgressions, and we a victim of our dominance. How we see the world around us and our place in it will determine what we do to save it.

The photographers in the second division approach the landscape as a transcendental medium—one that encompasses romantic as well as spiritual experiences. Nature/landscape to photographers like Ansel Adams, Minor White, and Paul Caponigro exemplifies purity of form, and a requiem for peace and tranquility. To poet and essayist Mary Oliver it is a personal landscape, with its familiar and consistent terrain that sustains a spiritual and emotional equilibrium. She laments, "It is one of the perils of our so-called civilized age that we do not acknowledge enough, or cherish enough, this connection between soul and landscape—between our own best possibilities, and the view from our own windows."

In the third section, nature/landscape is imbued with social and political significance. Man's encounters with the landscape reflect encroachment and disregard, as both aesthetic and ecological disaster lurk in the background. This is the prevailing spirit in the work of Robert Adams, Lewis Baltz, Frank Gohlke, Richard Misrach, and Marilyn Bridges. Author Tony Hiss writes on "the experience of place" and its impact on our daily lives. He points out that "the danger, as we are now beginning to see, is that whenever we make changes in our surroundings, we can too easily short-change ourselves. Over-development and urban sprawl can damage our lives as much as they damage our cities and countryside."

The fourth section is introduced by art critic and essayist Lucy R. Lippard, who discusses the impact of a creative and spiritual climate on contemporary landscape photography, and focuses on the so-called postmodern element in its midst—photographers like Tseng Kwong Chi, who self-consciously intervene in or thrust themselves upon the land, or who alter the landscape in some manner like Jerry N. Uelsmann, Walter De Maria, and Sally Mann. Lippard observes that revisionist theory and the "less-than-god-given modern incarnations" of nature, infused with social and environmental implications, have incited new interpretations by photographers, though she notes that "the dilemma of meaning" often obscures their intentions. And yet, through the artistry of these photographers, qualities of spirit can still be experienced through their work.

Gratitude is expressed to all who have worked on this issue, especially to Dr. John Rohrbach, Associate Curator of Photographs at the Amon Carter Museum, who helped to initiate the project, and who benefited this issue with his research skills and vision.

—THE EDITORS

Lynn Davis, *Horseshoe Falls*, 1992

Carleton E. Watkins, Untitled, n.d.

The whole of nature is a metaphor of the human mind.
—Ralph Waldo Emerson, from "Nature," 1836

POSTNATURAL

BY BILL McKIBBEN

What on earth are we looking at when we look at nature? Something separate from us, something removed? Or something of which we're a part? That is the original paradox for our species, a question that's been in the back of our collective mind since our earliest ancestors climbed down from the trees and began the process of confusing our relationship with everything else.

But now, in our lifetimes, this cliché of the millennia has taken on an unexpected new valence, an urgency. In the last few decades we've grown large enough as a species that something deep has changed. The possibility of this deep change dates from the atom bomb, I suppose—all of a sudden we were big enough to kill off ourselves and nature. We've backed away from that brink, thank God, but it turns out there are other thresholds. For instance, our profligate use of fossil fuel has by now altered the earth's atmosphere. Each square meter of the globe's surface now receives an additional two watts of solar energy. That doesn't sound like much, but it's enough to change everything. Data published in the last eighteen months shows that severe storms occur 20 percent more often than they did a century ago, that spring comes a week earlier to the northern hemisphere, that alpine glaciers and arctic permafrost are steadily melting.

And it's not just global warming. We've used so much nitrogen for fertilizer that we've altered the basic nutrient balance of rivers and bays. We wipe out hundreds of species a month. This is not the normal and unavoidable "pollution" that comes from altering the places where we live and grow our food. This is total. In a special issue of *Science* magazine last summer, four highly regarded researchers, including the president of the American Academy for the Advancement of Science, declared that we now lived on a "human-dominated" planet. This is new. We have ended nature.

And by ending nature we've answered in some way that original paradox. We are very much a part of nature—but no longer a subsidiary part like every other creature. We are everywhere. Every cubic meter of air carries our autograph—the telltale accumulation of carbon dioxide from the engines of our cars, the smokestacks of our factories, the combustion of our forests. An alien astronomer, by analyzing our changing atmosphere, would be able to gauge how much we consume. We set the level of the ocean by the size of our economies, the length of the seasons by how carelessly we live. If we wise up we can still limit our damage. But we've stumbled blindly across some perceptual boundary, and the world will never look the same to us as it once did. We show up in every frame now, carving our initials in the trunk of every redwood, painting the names of our fraternities on every Sierra cliff.

Oddly, though, we now enter a period when the forces of the natural world will matter more to us than they ever have before. Though every year of our history as a species has been marked—one place or another—by drought, flood, hurricane, fire, earthquake, volcano, our planet as a whole has been remarkably stable overall. Our civilization has been built on that physical stability; that lack of variation has allowed us to harvest, to build, to plan with a confidence so basic it goes unspoken.

Now that confidence will be shaken. By disturbing our climate, we alter every terrestrial force: wind speed, evaporation, rainfall. The world is becoming less reliable, more variable. And that will eventually alter our perception of nature. As it gets scarier (733 people died in one Chicago heat wave two summers ago), it will be easy to retreat to a view of nature as enemy and adversary. And as we come to see just how profoundly our greed and folly have shaped the world around us, it will be easy to concoct a postmodern, distanced sense of nature.

What we need instead is an unblinking willingness to confront painful reality, to locate us in our actual—tragic—relation to the earth. To do so would require understanding just how beautiful the earth still is, how gorgeous it remains even in its defaced state. And from that we need to construct a new art that would help us understand what it means to be human now. This century, unfortunately, has already forced such reconstructions on us—the Holocaust and AIDS are poignant and tragic examples. New ways of seeing have helped us, at least a little, to continue living amidst great sadness.

And this new way of seeing people and nature must help us in our doing as well, must help us to more than imagine what it might be like to take up less space, to reduce our dominion. The relation of the human and the natural is now both the key practical and the key aesthetic or moral question of our day. ■

F. J. Haynes, Cascades of the Columbia, scenery along the Northern Pacific Railroad, 1885

Timothy O'Sullivan, Lake in extinct volcanic crater, Arizona, 1871

In the morning I found, to my disgust, that the camp was to retain its position for another day.
I dreaded its languor and monotony, and to escape it, I set out to explore the surrounding
mountains. . . . After advancing for some time . . . I saw at some distance the black head and red
shoulders of an Indian among the bushes above. . . . Looking for a while at the old man, I was
satisfied that he was engaged in an act of worship, or prayer, or communion of some kind with

a supernatural being. . . . He has a guardian spirit, on whom he relies for succor and guidance. To him all nature is instinct with mystic influence. Among those mountains not a wild beast was prowling, a bird singing, or a leaf fluttering, that might not tend to direct his destiny, or give warning of what was in store for him; and he watches the world of nature around him as the astrologer watches the stars. —Francis Parkman, from *The Oregon Trail*, 1849

Carleton E. Watkins, The
Summit of Lasens Butte,
1870, from the album
"California Views," 1876

Here was a poem he knew . . . but it wasn't a poem, it was a song. His mother sang it often, working at the sewing machine in winter. . . . As he sang the trace grew on him again, he lost himself entirely. The bright hard dividing lines between senses blurred,

View of the McClure Company album
showing Hallat Peak, Bear Lake and Sheep Mountain, Estes Park, Colorado, n.d.

and buttercups, smell of primrose, feel of hard gravel under body and elbows, sight of the ghosts of mountains haunting the southern horizon, were one intensely felt experience focused by the song the book had evoked.—Wallace Stegner, from *Big Rock Candy Mountain*

Herman F. Nielson, Frozen Niagara Falls, ca. 1885

William Henry Jackson, Mammoth Hot Springs, 1878

Perhaps it is necessary for me to try these places, perhaps it is my destiny to know the world. It only excites the outside of me. The inside it leaves more isolated and stoic than ever. That's how it is. It is all a form of running away from oneself and the great problems: all this wild west.

—D. H. Lawrence, from a letter written to Catherine Carowell

Evelyn J. Cameron, The four-foot-high-by-three-and-a-half-foot-wide nest
of a red-tailed hawk atop a high pillar of rock, near Great Falls, n.d.

Unknown Photographer, Photograph from the "San Carlo Ranch Album," n.d.

Lifting his head, he saw how the prairie beyond the fireguard looked darker than in dry times, healthier with green-brown tints, smaller and more intimate somehow than it did when the heat waves crawled over scorched grass and carried the horizons backward into dim and unseeable distances. And standing in the yard above his one clean footprint, feeling his own verticality in all that spread of horizontal land, he sensed that as the prairie shrank he grew. He was immense. A little jump would crack his head on the sky; a stride would take him to any horizon.

—Wallace Stegner, from *Big Rock Candy Mountain*

HOME

BY MARY OLIVER

A certain lucent correspondence has served me, all my life, in the ongoing search for my deepest thoughts and feelings. It is the relationship of my own mind to landscape, to the physical world—especially to that part of it with which, over the years, I have (and not casually) become intimate. It is no great piece of furniture in the universe—no Niagara, or rainforest, or Sahara. Yet it is beautiful, and it ripples in the weathers as lively as any outpouring from the Great Lakes.

In its minor turns, and tinsels, and daily changes, this landscape seems actually intent on providing pleasure, as indeed it does; in its *constancy*, its inexorable obedience to laws I cannot begin to imagine much less understand, it is a still richer companion—steady commentary against my own lesser moods—my flightiness, my indifferences, my mind- and heart-absences.

I mean, by such flightiness, something that feels unsatisfied at the center of my life—that makes me shaky, fickle, inquisitive, and hungry. I could call it a longing for home and not be far wrong. Or I could call it a longing for whatever supercedes, if it cannot pass through, understanding. Other words that come to mind: faith, grace, rest. In my outward appearance and life habits I hardly change—there's never been a day that my friends haven't been able to say, and at a distance, "There's Oliver, still standing around in the weeds. There she is, still scribbling in her notebook." But, at the center: I am shaking; I am flashing like tinsel. Restless. I read about ideas. Yet I let them remain ideas. I read about the poet who threw his books away, the better to come to a spiritual completion. Yet I keep my books. I flutter; I am attentive, maybe I even rise a little, balancing; then I fall back.

I don't however despair of such failures! I know I am sister to the dreamy-hearted dog who thinks only small thoughts; and to the green tree who thinks no thoughts at all, as well as to Rumi, and St. Francis. No, I don't mind the failures so long as I am still striving.

Which I am, and in this way. Daily I walk out across my landscape, the same fields, the same woods, and the same pale beaches; I stand beside the same blue and festive sea where the invisible winds, on late summer afternoons, are wound into huge tense

Minor White, *Grand Tetons*, Wyoming, 1959

As I become more in harmony with the world around, through, and in me, the varieties of time weave together. Chronological time, the time my psyche takes, and creative time were once always at odds with each other. Less so now that the manifestations of inner growth are seen to be set in my path as if by an invisible disincarnate friend. When I have sensed his presence, the photographs, afterward, seem like footprints . . . his or mine is the question!

—Minor White

Koichiro Kurita, *Fall*, Connecticut, 1991

coils, and the waves put on their white feathers and begin to leap shoreward, to their last screaming and throbbing landfall. Times beyond remembering I have seen such moments: summer falling to fall, to be followed by what will follow: winter again: count on it. Opulent and ornate world, because at its root, and its axis, and its ocean bed, it swings through the universe *quietly* and *certainly*. It is: fun, and familiar, and healthful, and unbelievably refreshing, and lovely. And it is the theater of the spiritual; it is the multiform utterly obedient to a mystery.

And here I build a platform, and live upon it, and think my thoughts, and aim high. To rise, I must have a field to rise from. To deepen, I must have a bedrock from which to descend. The constancy of the physical world, under its green and blue dyes, draws me toward a better, richer self, call it elevation (there is hardly an adequate word), where I might ascend a little—where a gloss of spirit would mirror itself in worldly action. I don't mean just mild goodness. I mean feistiness too, the fires of human energy stoked; I mean a gladness vivacious enough to disarrange the sorrows of the world into something better. I mean whatever real rejoicing can do! We all know how brassy and wonderful it is to come into some new understanding. Imagine what it would be like, to lounge on the high ledge of submission and pure wonder. Nature, all around us, is our manifest exemplar. Not from the fox, or the leaf, or the drop of rain will you ever hear doubt or argument.

People say to me: wouldn't you like to see Yosemite? The Bay of Fundy? The Brooks Range? I smile and answer, "Oh yes—sometime," and go off to my woods, my ponds, my sun-filled harbor, no more than a blue comma on the map of the world but, to me, the emblem of everything. It is the intimate, never the general, that is teacherly. The idea of love is not love. The idea of ocean is neither salt nor sand; the face of the seal cannot rise from the *idea* to stare at you, to astound your heart. Time must grow thick and merry with incident, before thought can begin.

It is one of the perils of our so-called civilized age that we do not yet acknowledge enough, or cherish enough, this connection between soul and landscape—between our own best possibilities, and the view from our own windows. We need the world as much as it needs us, and we need it in privacy, intimacy, and surety. We need the field from which the lark rises—bird that is more than itself, that is the voice of the universe: vigorous, godly joy. Without the physical world such hope is: hacked off. Is: dried up. Without wilderness no fish could leap and flash, no deer could bound soft as eternal waters over the field; no bird could fly. Nor could we. ∎

For millennia, water lay over the land. Untold generations of water plants, birds, animals, insects, lived, shed bits of themselves, and died. I used to like to imagine how it all drifted down, lazily, in the warm, soupy water—leaves, seeds, feathers, scales, flesh, bones, petals, pollen—then mixed with the saturated soil below and became, itself, soil . . . and the soil was the treasure, thicker, richer, more alive with a past and future abundance of life than any soil anywhere.

—Jane Smiley, from
A Thousand Acres

Robert Dawson, *Untitled #1*,
from the "Mono Lake Series," 1979

David Gibson, *Cloud March*, Fort Davis, Texas, 1988

To the attentive eye, each moment of the year has its own beauty, and in the same field, it beholds, every hour, a picture which was never seen before, and which shall never be seen again. The heavens change every moment, and reflect their glory or gloom on the plains beneath.
—Ralph Waldo Emerson, from "Nature," 1836

William Clift, *Rainbow*, Waldo,
New Mexico, 1978

Paul Caponigro, *Sky, Near Dixon, New Mexico*, 1977

Peter Gasser, *Big Sur, California,* 1979

Of all my photographs, the ones that have the most meaning for me are those I was moved to make from a certain vantage point, at a certain moment and no other, and for which I did not draw on my abilities to fabricate a picture, composition-wise or otherwise. You might say that I was taken in. . . . I have always felt after such experiences that there was more than myself involved. It is not chance. It happens often. In looking back at a particular picture and trying to recall the experience that led to it, that inexplicable element is still present. I have no other way to express what I mean, other than to say that more than myself is present. —Paul Caponigro

Brett Weston, *Mono Lake,
California*, 1957

38

Dorothea Lange, *The Road West, New Mexico*, 1938

I am waiting
for a rebirth of wonder
and I am waiting for someone
to really discover America
and wail
and I am waiting
for the discovery
of a new symbolic western frontier. . . .

—Lawrence Ferlinghetti, from
A Coney Island of the Mind

THE EXPERIENCE OF PLACE

BY TONY HISS

We all react, consciously and unconsciously, to the places where we live and work, in ways we scarcely notice or that are only now becoming known to us. Ever-accelerating changes in most people's day-to-day circumstances are helping us and prodding us, sometimes forcing us, to learn that our ordinary surroundings, built and natural alike, have an immediate and a continuing effect on the way we feel and act, and on our health and intelligence. These places have an impact on our sense of self, our sense of safety, the kind of work we get done, the ways we interact with other people, even our ability to function as citizens in a democracy. In short, the places where we spend our time affect the people we are and can become.

As places around us change—both the communities that shelter us and the larger regions that support them—we all undergo changes inside. This means that whatever we experience in a place is both a serious environmental issue and a deeply personal one. Our relationship with the places we know and meet up with—where you are right now; and where you've been earlier today; and wherever you'll be in another few hours—is a close bond, intricate in nature, and not abstract, not remote at all: It's enveloping, almost a continuum with all we are and think. And the danger, as we are now beginning to see, is that whenever we make changes in our surroundings, we can all too easily shortchange ourselves, by cutting ourselves off from some of the sights or sounds, the shapes or textures, or other information from a place that have helped mold our understanding and are now necessary for us to thrive. Overdevelopment and urban sprawl can damage our own lives as much as they damage our cities and countryside.

The way to avoid the danger is to start doing three things at once: Make sure that when we change a place, the change agreed upon nurtures our growth as capable and responsible people, protects the natural environment, and developes jobs and homes enough for all.

Although we have always prided ourselves on our willingness to adapt to all habitats, and on our skill at prospering and making ourselves comfortable wherever we are—in a meadow, in a desert, on the tundra, or out on the ocean—we don't just adapt to places, or modify them in order to ease our burdens. We're the only species that over and over has deliberately transformed our surroundings in order to stretch our capacity for understanding and provoke new accomplishments.

Luckily, we have a hidden ally—or, if not hidden, at least a long-neglected, overlooked, undervalued one. This ally is our built-in ability to experience places directly, an ability that makes it possible for people to know personally, through their own senses, about many of the ways our surroundings work within us. Paying careful attention to our experiences of places, we can use our own responses, thoughts, and feelings to help us replenish the places we love.

We can experience any place because we've all received, as part of the structure of our attention, a mechanism that drinks in whatever it can from our surroundings. This underlying awareness—I call it simultaneous perception—seems to operate continuously, at least during waking hours. While normal waking consciousness works to simplify perception, allowing us to act quickly and flexibly by helping us remain seemingly oblivious to almost everything except the task in front of us, simultaneous perception is more like an extra, or a sixth, sense: It broadens and diffuses the beam of attention evenhandedly across all the senses so we can take in whatever is around us—which means sensations of touch and balance, for instance, in addition to all sights, sounds, and smells.

Anytime we make conscious use of simultaneous perception, we can add on to our thinking. . . . It's simultaneous perception that allows any of us a direct sense of continuing membership in our communities, and our regions, and the fellowship of all living creatures.

Until recently, when people spoke about a vivid experience of a place, it would usually be a wonderful memory, a magic moment at one of the sweet spots of the world. These days people often tell me that some of their most unforgettable experiences of places are disturbingly painful and have to do with unanticipated loss. Sometimes there's less to see or hear or do in a place: A curving road in front of an old suburban house, for instance, gets straightened and widened, and suddenly a favorite grove of oaks or pines

Lewis Baltz, *Prospector Village, Subdivision Phase III, Lot 55, looking West*, 1981

Art Sinsabaugh, *top to bottom: Midwest Landscape #7*, 1961. *Midwest Landscape #64*, 1962.
Midwest Landscape #33, 1961. *Midwest Landscape #29*, 1961.

*First there are the broken things—myself and others. I don't mind that—I'm gone—shot to pieces.
I'm part of the scheme—I'm the broken end of a song myself. We are all that, here in the West, here
in Chicago. Tongues clatter against teeth. There's nothing but shrill screams and a rattle. That had
to be—it's part of the scheme.* —Sherwood Anderson, from "Song of Industrial America"

Joan Myers, *110 Mile Station*, Kansas, 1983

Frank Gohlke, *Grain Elevators and Lightning Flash*, Lamesa, Texas, 1975

Lonelyness, thy other name,
thy one true synonym, is prairie.

—William A. Quayle,
from *The Prairie and*
the Sea, 1905

Marilyn Bridges, *Isolation Farmhouse*,
Greer County, Oklahoma, 1987

Stuart Klipper, Cattle and storage bins off highway 232, Hill County, Montana, 1995

Lois Conner, *Glacier Point, Yosemite National Park*, 1984

Robert Glenn Ketchum, *New Hamburg Boat Marina*, 1983

Wanda Hammerbeck, *A Point of Vulnerability in the American West*, 1997

One learns a landscape finally not by knowing the name or identity of everything in it, but by perceiving the relationships in it—like that between the sparrow and the twig. The difference between the relationships and the elements is the same as that between written history and a catalog of events.
           —Barry Lopez, from
              Crossing Open Ground

Virginia Beahan and Laura McPhee, *Foundation of a Burned House*, Carbon Canyon, California, 1995

Nancy Goldring, *Wanwood: Trees*, 1992

Philipp Scholz Rittermann, Diptych, *top*: *Seagull, La Jolla Cove*, La Jolla, California, 1991;
bottom: *Half-Dome from Washburn Point*, Yosemite, California, 1989

Tseng Kwong Chi, *clockwise from top left*:
Grand Canyon, Arizona, 1987. *Monument Valley, Arizona*, 1987.
Grand Canyon, Arizona, 1987. *Grand Canyon, Arizona*, 1987.

Walter De Maria, *Lightning Field*, 1977. Photograph by John Cliett, 1979

SEVENTY YEARS LATER

It is an illusion that we were ever alive,
Lived in the houses of mothers, arranged ourselves
By our own motions in a freedom of air.

Regard the freedom of seventy years ago.
It is no longer air. The houses still stand,
Though they are rigid in rigid emptiness.

Even our shadows, their shadows, no longer remain.
The lives these lived in the mind are at an end.
They never were . . . The sounds of the guitar

Were not and are not. Absurd. The words spoken
Were not and are not. It is not to be believed.
The meeting at noon at the edge of the field seems like

An invention, an embrace between one desperate clod
And another in a fantastic consciousness,
In a queer assertion of humanity:

A theorem proposed between the two—
Two figures in a nature of the sun,
In the sun's design of its own happiness,

As if nothingness contained a métier,
A vital assumption, an impermanence
In its permanent cold, an illusion so desired

That the green leaves came and covered the high rock,
That the lilacs came and bloomed, like a blindness cleaned,
Exclaiming bright sight, as it was satisfied,

In a birth of sight. The blooming and the musk
Were being alive, an incessant being alive,
A particular of being, that gross universe.

—Wallace Stevens, from "The Rock"

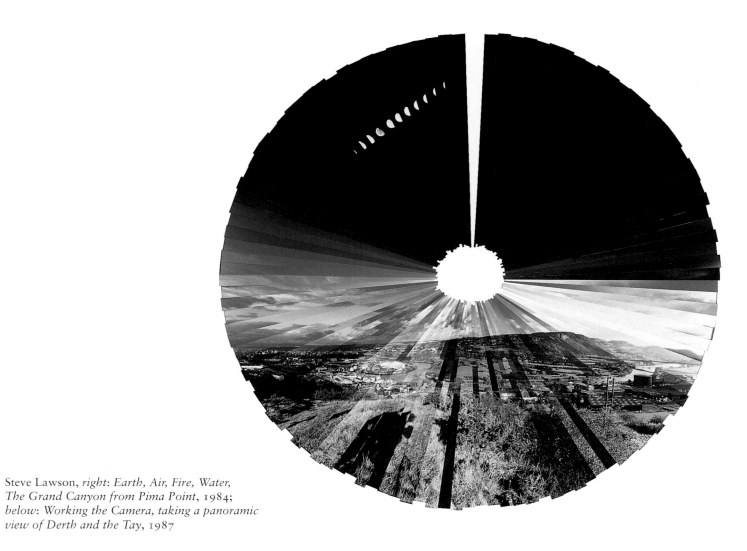

Steve Lawson, *right*: Earth, Air, Fire, Water,
The Grand Canyon from Pima Point, 1984;
below: Working the Camera, *taking a panoramic
view of Derth and the Tay*, 1987

Barbara Kasten,
*Black Canyon,
Arizona,* 1994

Edward Weston, *Hot Coffee*,
Mojave Desert, 1937

lived for centuries cut down by the fire of the desert. Desert photography, however, tends to look wet with its obsession with exceptional wildflower displays during weird periods of moisture, its focus on springs, water holes, and giant close-ups of lubricious cactus flowers, its lust for thunderheads and lightning displays. If you want to die, get up early when a rare snowstorm coats the Sonoran Desert and get between a white covered saguaro and the stampede of desert photographers.

Those are the sacred ten points of desert photography. I have no real quarrel with them; any cult has a right to its house rules. For most of this century, it has created a special place, a desert that we imagine because we are afraid to look at ourselves and so go to the desert and use it as a magic mirror. But like any cult, desert photography is self-limiting, it is only of value to fellow communicants, those who already believe the rules. And, like any cult, it is an act of self-mutilation, in this case a ritual plucking out of the eyes, a willful blindness in the bright white light of the sun. Cults are useful to us because they protect us from experience. For most of this century the cult of desert photography has numbed us so that about the only desert we can recognize is a Cibachrome.

I'll tell you a little story, a parable, that is outside the official sacred texts of the cult and also is questionable because it really happened. A year ago, I agreed to write some of this nature stuff for a publisher who would then use wads of my scribbling to provide a kind of verbal compost heap upon which to festoon landscape photographs. As part of this ugly task, I walked for over thirty miles through the rock and heat of Bryce Canyon National Park during a June drought. The land was tinder dry and the rangers feared the slightest spark would burn down their factory of nature worship, an industrial site that they referred to when deep in their cups as a "national sacrifice area." The park itself is a green smear of conifers on a tongue of sandstone known as the Colorado Plateau, a cooler desert that has devoured a generation's Kodachromes and has become the pinup rockpile of numerous airports and hotels.

Bryce is a shrine to love of the land. Its zany spires draw souls from around the world who worship what baser human beings might call erosion. For three days I walked the backcountry of Bryce and during that time I ran into three people. Two of these people were a couple, plunked down about a mile from the trailhead and from the glazed look in their eyes not likely to soon rise from their nuptial ground. The third was the real McCoy, a German twenty miles from nowhere plodding toward nowhere. This low turnout for the gritty face of nature is typical of the cult I have been describing. Nature worship no longer requires nature. We have ascended to a higher plane, Virtual Nature. Here are the numbers: 1.6 million people visit Bryce each year, almost all of them during a few temperate months of summer when the park, squatting at 8,000 to 9,000 feet, is free of snow. Recently, the park highway had to be widened to accommodate tour buses and herds of Winnebagos. Commercial helicopter lights whisk the faithful over the spires from dawn to dusk, seven days a week. Of the 1.6 million visitors, three hundred walk up to the counter in the park headquarters and ask for a permit so that they can get out of their cars and walk away from a road.

These numbers are a testament to our keeping of the faith. Seldom has a cult had such a disciplined adherence to its Ten Commandments as desert photography. The only group I have ever encountered that is remotely as disciplined are pornography freaks who, like the desert photography cult members, are incapable of being bored and can look at the exact same images over and over and over. The only venue I know of that is as dedicated to avoidance of experience as a designated natural viewpoint on a scenic highway is a topless bar. In both instances, the communicants have a deep dread of risk and a deep need for the comfort of predictable events. And in both instances, the faithful insist to each other that at last they are looking at the real thing.

I am reconciled to being one of the unsaved, one of the unwashed. I'll take my deserts like my breasts, as they come, not as they are framed. I will continue to be surprised, threatened, hot, torn, and thirsty. No doubt when I die I will go to the hell of the unfaithful to spend all of eternity surrounded by white light, soft flesh, thorns, and a hot pan of dirt where a woman beckons. I have been forewarned that hell is shy of water. And Cibachrome. And I will stumble, alas, over the Ten Commandments of the cult. I never was very good at the original Ten Commandments for that matter.

Desert photography will continue to have an imaginary life of its own, much like American foreign policy. No one to my knowledge connects American foreign policy with the real world. Instead, it is savored for its sheer exuberance in describing a fantasy land of free global trade, emerging democracies that love Mickey Mouse, evil empires that must be Star Warred and the importance of human rights—rights that conveniently stop at the door of, say, a Nike sneaker factory. I am sure that around the planet the black humor of American foreign policy gives at least as much entertainment value as American movies.

Just so with desert photography. Across the vast bosom of our republic it will continue to succor sensitive souls as they contemplate their Volvos and listen to CDs of humpback whale doo-wop groups. Like drugs, desert photography is an inevitable and essential part of our deadened civilization. It means never having to open our eyes. ■

THE BUZZ ABOUT PAPARAZZI:
MARCELLO MASTROIANNI REMEMBERS WORKING WITH FEDERICO FELLINI AND TAZIO SECCHIAROLI, THE FIRST PAPARAZZO

A previously unpublished, exclusive *Aperture* interview with the Italian actor.

By Gloria Satta

pp. 77–78: Tazio Secchiaroli's photographs taken on the set of *8½.*

Marcello Mastroianni did not collect photographs. "It would make me think of the past, and I don't want to. I'm like an old whore: when I'm finished with one trick, here I am, ready for the next." The actor, who died in December 1996, three years after this interview took place, did not even have a copy of Tazio Secchiaroli's famous photo from the set of Federico Fellini's *8½*: Marcello, shirtless, a sheet wound about his flanks, a hat on his head and a whip in his hand. The figure of a "mythological cowboy," who would enter our collective imagination as the very symbol of Fellini's filmmaking. "No, the past is always behind me. I live in the present and the future."

And thus, Mastroianni spoke of Fellini in the present, as though he were still alive: "Federico wants . . . ," "Federico likes. . . ." The actor was the protagonist of five films of the director—who passed away on October 31, 1993, shortly before this interview took place—and ultimately came to be identified with him, defined universally as "Fellini's alter ego." Marcello appeared in *La Dolce Vita* (1960); *8½* (1963); *The City of Women* (1985); *Ginger and Fred* (1985); and *Intervista* (1987). It was on the set of *La Dolce Vita* that Mastroianni first met the photographer Tazio Secchiaroli.

GLORIA SATTA: Do you remember that first meeting?

MARCELLO MASTROIANNI: Yes, Federico introduced us. Tazio was involved then, shooting photographs, I believe he was doing a special report on the film, and was an advisor for the character of "Paparazzo." He had a considerable knowledge of the material, even though at that point he was no longer really a paparazzi photographer, but dedicated to true and proper photography, with great results.

SATTA: Were there a lot of paparazzi in those days?

MASTROIANNI: Yes, I think so, even though they weren't bothering me because I wasn't famous, so they didn't pester me. They went along the Via Veneto in Rome doing their work, and they were already very pushy.

SATTA: You were never very fond of them, were you?

MASTROIANNI: Eventually, they made my life impossible. They played horrible tricks on me, like when Chiara—my daughter with Catherine Deneuve—was born. They went to the registrar's office in Paris and photographed a false document that "proved" that I refused to recognize the baby. Really disgraceful! Even today, when I see a paparazzo I can't help associating him with dirty journalism, an offense to human dignity. But Tazio was always different, a truly sweet person, a great professional creator of magnificent photographs. And, like me, he was very privileged because he was in Fellini's good books, and was able to stay close to him.

SATTA: Was the director Fellini inspired by Secchiaroli to create the [Paparazzo] character in *La Dolce Vita*?

MASTROIANNI: Yes, I believe so. The word "paparazzo" came from Fellini's fantasy, and he was constantly creating nicknames for us. He called me "Snaporaz," and I called him "Callaghan." We played together like a pair of kids.

SATTA: How did you meet Fellini?

MASTROIANNI: In 1959, we were introduced by his wife Giulietta [Masina], with whom I had worked in the theater. He was looking for the main character in *La Dolce Vita*, and we met on the beach at Ostia. "The producer wants to give me Paul Newman," he said, "but I'd prefer a more anonymous actor, someone with a face like yours."

SATTA: And what did you say?

MASTROIANNI: I asked innocently, "Can I read for the part?" I didn't know that at the time with Fellini, there were no scripts, and there never would be. He turned to Ennio Flajano, who was with us and said, "Ennio, show Marcello the script." The writer presented me with a piece of paper, a drawing of a man with an enormous phallus, surrounded by Sirens; like in an Esther Williams water ballet. That was it: that was the entire production plan for the film. And that was the way Fellini treated you, like a baby. But actors are babies. And that embarrassing drawing was the start of my long game with Fellini. He was the easiest director I ever worked with in my career.

SATTA: Why easy?

MASTROIANNI: Because all you had to do was follow his direction, to go along with his genius, without worrying about studying a part or a script. His films were born during a car-ride, or from a chat between us, or during a lunch on the

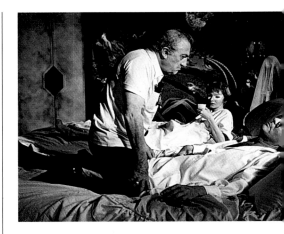

invented in the moment: there were no questions to ask and no answers to expect. This is why he tried with so many foreign actors, but kept coming back to me: they wanted explanations, while I always accepted his game. Some even cried.

SATTA: Like who?

MASTROIANNI: Anouk Amiée. During the work on *La Dolce Vita*, she often burst into tears: "Fellini asked me to change a line, but why? Why?" She didn't understand that an actor, with him, had to be a marionette, ready to be maneuvered, with happiness and gaiety. By contrast, I had fun with it. But what explanations, what tests! In his films, I was a spectator even before being an actor. I accepted even his irony, which could sometimes be ferocious, or downright cruel.

SATTA: Cruel?

MASTROIANNI: Yes. During the retakes of *8½*, in the scene where I take a bath in the tub, I asked him not to shoot my legs: they were very skinny, and I was ashamed of them. So he made me wrap myself in a sheet like a gaucho. And then, he made one of the women who were circling me say this line: "But look at him, what skinny legs!"

SATTA: Which is your favorite film?

MASTROIANNI: *8½*, without question. When I see it as a spectator, it still makes me very emotional. It brings back the failure of that generation, from which we were expecting so much, and which instead amounted to so little. . . .

SATTA: Is it true that Fellini wanted you to be thin and kept putting you on diets?

MASTROIANNI: Not on diets exactly, but when we were in production, during breaks, he'd send me a masseur to prevent me from eating. He wanted me to be beautiful, and so he appealed to the director of photography Peppino [Giuseppe] Rotunno: "Marcello's nose is too short, do something about it!" Federico had an attention for actors that I've only come across in one other director: Luchino Visconti. But Visconti was a very authoritative figure whom you felt protected by, almost in awe of, while Federico was like

the kid at school whom you'd ask: "Could I copy your homework?"

SATTA: Was this complicity between you only in your working relationship?

MASTROIANNI: No, it was really in every part of life. I had the great privilege to be his friend, his brother, his . . . lover. During the production of *La Dolce Vita*, Giulietta was in Poland making a film. So I moved in with Fellini. In the morning, he'd leave first, but before he left, he'd bring me coffee in bed. "Please Marcellino," he'd say, "don't go back to sleep." Once, I was heading back to the set of *8½*, and on the street, I ran into an incredibly beautiful woman, who gave me a big smile. When I got to Fellini's place and told him about it, he got upset with me for not having followed her. He said to me, "Okay, while I change the camera setup, go on back to her, but hurry up. We'll wait for you before we start shooting again. . . ."

SATTA: If Fellini hadn't been a director, what do you think he would have been?

MASTROIANNI: Certainly a writer. He loved telling stories. He was spellbinding.

SATTA: And what relationship did he have with photography?

MASTROIANNI: A very creative relationship. He liked the paparazzi and loved to improvise, and followed the "attack work" of those photographers with great interest. Like Fellini, they were creators. And Fellini, like the paparazzi, had a lot of fun. ■

Translated from the Italian by Marguerite Shore.

beach at Fregene. And when we were shooting, I'd arrive on the set in the morning. "What gorgeous people, Federico, what should I do today?" "What seems right to you? A poem. Youth is so beautiful, but always slipping away. . . . We can make all the adjustments when we do the dubbing." And that's what would happen. While they were shooting, the extras didn't say lines, but numbers: thirteen, seventy-two, ninety-five. . . . Even Guido Alberti, who played the producer in *8½*, did this. And Fellini was right: the cinema is a marvelous falsehood, it is an art that can lie at any moment.

SATTA: Have you found any other directors who work this way?

MASTROIANNI: No, never. The improvisation that really reigned with Fellini would have been unthinkable for any other director. For example on an American set, where everything is rigidly set up and scientifically planned, nothing is left to chance. With Federico, it was all

CONTRIBUTORS

CHARLES BOWDEN is the author of fourteen books including *Blood Orchid: An Unnatural History of America* and *Desierto: Memories of the Future*. He is a contributing editor of *Esquire*, and also writes for other magazines such as *Harper's* and the *New York Times Book Review*, as well as for newspapers.

THOMAS BRIDGES is a writer and is the guest editor for this issue. His work has appeared in many newspapers and magazines, including the *New York Times*, *Chicago Tribune*, *McCall's*, and *Parabola*. He has been a contributing editor for several books on landscape photography. Bridges is presently completing a trilogy of performance plays.

TONY HISS was a staff writer for the *New Yorker* for over twenty years and has authored seven books, including *The Experience of Place,* and coauthored *All Aboard with E. M. Frimbo*. In 1995, the National Recreation and Park Association awarded Hiss its National Literary Award for a lifetime of writing on the environment, travel, and landscape and their impact on American lives.

LUCY R. LIPPARD's seventeen published books include *Overlay: Contemporary Art and the Art of Prehistory* and *Partial Recall: Photographs of Native North Americans*. She has been a columnist for the *Village Voice*, *In These Times*, and *Z Magazine*. Lippard's most recent book is *The Lure of the Local: Senses of Place in a Multicentered Society*.

BILL McKIBBEN is the author of *The End of Nature*, *The Age of Missing Information*, and most recently, *Hope, Human and Wild*. A former staff writer for the *New Yorker*, he has written on nature and environmental subjects for dozens of national publications, including the *Atlantic Monthly* and *Rolling Stone*.

MARY OLIVER has written over ten books of poetry and essays, and has received both the Pulitzer Prize for Poetry and the National Book Award. Her newest book is *West Wind, a book of poems*. *Rules for the Dance: A Handbook for Writing and Reading Metrical Verse* will be published next spring. Oliver is on the faculty of Bennington College and holds the Catherine Osgood Foster Chair for Distinguished Teaching.

GLORIA SATTA is a journalist living in Rome.

ERRATA

In *Aperture 148*, *Delirium*, the artists Marcia Lippman and David LaChapelle should have had their names spelled as such.

Also in *Delirium*, the photograph on page 77, reproduced from the greeting card on which it appears and which the accompanying  article discusses, was inadvertently printed without out proper attribution. The name of the photographer is Karin Rosenthal and the image is titled *Belly Landscape*, 1980. The greeting card is copyright © 1994 by the Borealis Press Inc.

CREDITS

Appearing in DoubleTake

Mary Berridge

Debbie Fleming Caffery

Paul D'Amato

Wendy Ewald

Larry Fink

Lee Friedlander

William Gedney

Helen Levitt

Danny Lyon

Joel Meyerowitz

Richard Misrach

Nicholas Nixon

Gilles Peress

Thomas Roma

Judith Joy Ross

John Szarkowski

Larry Towell

and others

Photographed by William Gedney. © Special Collections Library, Duke University.

Pictures and words connect on their own.
That's why DoubleTake allows the photographs
we publish to speak for themselves. And why
we let the written word echo rather than
explain. DoubleTake is a vivid magazine for
visual readers. See for yourself. For a no-risk
trial subscription, call 1-800-234-0981, ext 57091.
One year (4 issues) $19.

DoubleTake
See for yourself.